GRIT & Bear It!
ACTIVITY GUIDE

Activities to Engage, Encourage
and Inspire Perseverance

for Grades 5-10

Press

Boys Town, Nebraska

Written by **Tamara Zentic**, M.S.

Illustrated by **Lisa M. Griffin**

GRIT & Bear It! Activity Guide
Text and Illustrations Copyright © 2015 by Father Flanagan's Boys' Home
ISBN 978-1-934490-65-5

Published by Boys Town Press
14100 Crawford St.
Boys Town, Nebraska 68010

Printed in the United States
10 9 8 7 6 5 4 3 2 1

**For a Boys Town Press catalog, call 1-800-282-6657
or visit our website: BoysTownPress.org.**

Boys Town Press is the publishing division of Boys Town, a national organization serving children and families.

Table of Contents

BOYS TOWN NATIONAL HOTLINE®
1-800-448-3000
A crisis, resource, and referral number for kids and parents

Introduction

One of my favorite parts of the Olympics, or any major sporting event, is hearing the stories of the athletes and how they make it to the competition. Most of the stories are "grit lessons," waiting to inspire and motivate us. Time after time, I have heard the account of how an athlete overcame unthinkable odds or obstacles in order to succeed and compete at the highest level. The more obstacles or hardships an athlete overcomes or endures, the more we tend to cheer him or her on. Life is hard; we all want to be "overcomers" of our own life stories. That's why "stories of triumph" resonate with us. We find that our own struggles in life are eerily similar to those of others who have faced challenges. And for a brief moment in time, we are hopeful that we too can overcome our obstacles and hardships.

We typically don't know anything more about "underdog" athletes other than that, through their determination and perseverance, they are representing the achievement of dreams for many across the globe.

I suggest that this is one of the reasons why we are so fascinated with the Olympics and other major sporting events. These athletes possess GRIT, more GRIT than most of us have ever experienced. They have taken the difficult road. They have given relentless effort by rolling up their sleeves and getting dirty. They have given their sweat, tears, and time, and all they have inside of them.

There is a television show called "Shark Tank" that reflects this same concept. Hopeful entrepreneurs come on the show seeking big money to expand their businesses, which they've started through an invention or innovation they believe in. This program has gained popularity because it seems to represent the heart of the American Dream. America is known as the land of opportunity, and this show has capitalized on that by tapping into the dreams of ordinary

1

"…it allows students to develop life-long coping skills that will enhance their opportunities for success in all areas of their lives."

individuals. After watching several episodes, you start to pick out the "grittiest" entrepreneurs; those are the ones who, through their hard work, ideas, and singleness of purpose, are most often rewarded by landing a lucrative investment deal.

As average workers, we are drawn to these types of programs because we see some of our own dreams in these gritty entrepreneurs. We may have had the same idea, or know that we possess the resources or intelligence to succeed in inventing our own product or starting our own business. But we wonder if we would be able to "stay the course." We ask ourselves if we would have the inner drive, perseverance, dedication, or singleness of mind that it takes to achieve these goals. We wonder: Do I have the ability to make great personal sacrifices in order to delay gratification and finally achieve the admirable goals I've set for myself?

Yet, a bigger question we can ask as a society is, do the youth of today possess these qualities? Are the leaders of tomorrow going to be able to overcome great obstacles and "defy the odds"? Are we instilling the characteristics of grit into our homes, our classrooms, and our society?

The youth of today face challenges and hardships that are sometimes more difficult than those faced by previous generations. Couple that with the reality of living in an instantaneous society and you quickly realize the odds that are already rising up to meet our youth. Many seek immediate gratification, and the trend seems to be to "abandon ship" if the going gets too tough. Having

such a vast number of choices at their disposal appears to make it very easy for young people to simply change course and pursue something else for a while. So how do we ensure that our youth are going to develop those qualities that will enable them to overcome the unwelcome surprises that life will throw at them? How do we teach the importance of sacrifice and delaying gratification? It is from asking these questions that the book, *GRIT & Bear It!,* was conceived.

As the first piece in the *From Black & White to Living Color* series, *GRIT & Bear It!* is a short book that's an easy read for students, teachers, and parents. The words and the messages are straightforward, but there are also underlying questions and mindsets that are exposed and merit further exploration and discussion. The book is for anyone who would benefit from thinking about grit and using the strategies for obtaining more grit in his or her life. *GRIT & Bear It!* is for anyone who is facing hard times, obstacles, setbacks, or discouragement. It is for anyone who has been tempted to give in and take the instant, easy way out. My hope is that the book will prompt the individual who reads it to set out on a quest in search of "grit."

The book can be utilized as a stand-alone or in conjunction with the *GRIT & Bear It! Activity Guide,* which is a natural for any classroom. The lessons promote the development of more grit and enable students to self-evaluate how much grit they possess with regard to schoolwork, interactions with others, and class pursuits. Having grit has become an important issue for youth today.

In education, we are heavily focused on Core Academics and Standardized Testing. These two areas drive the school day, the school year, and the school purse strings. They appear to be the measure of accountability for students, teachers, and schools. Many efforts are being made to bring all students up to a "proficient" level, or better, in education. We review, and review, and then review some more. We have pep rallies and give out candy as incentives before a big standardized test and talk about the importance of the test. But when it is actually test time, we realize, as educators, that there are many variables we don't have any control over that will determine how well students perform on these important tests. We can't control a student's sleep or eating habits, home life, motivation, or the amount of effort he or she will devote to the task. Students might know they are expected to write five paragraphs for a state assessment, but they might decide to give up after writing only two. Why? How do we account for this? What other factors are in play when it comes to determining the level of success our youth will experience? If we simply choose to believe that academics and testing are the only things that determine how successful a student is or will be, then we are living in a "Black & White" world. *GRIT & Bear It!* and the *GRIT & Bear It! Activity Guide* are the first of a series of books and activities that introduce "Color" to the "Black & White" student and school setting. Using Executive Functions and Social Skills as additional indicators of success, we can add dimension to our students and tap into their reservoir of intangible potential. Their ability to persevere, to be optimistic, to have a zest for life, to explore their own curiosity, to get along better with others, to practice self-control, and to exhibit grit in their everyday lives is the self-motivating spark that pushes them to do their best, thus improving academic achievement and test scores. But more importantly, it allows students to develop life-long coping skills that will enhance their opportunities for success in all areas of their lives.

HOW TO USE THIS ACTIVITY GUIDE

This Activity Guide provides numerous ready-to-use activities you can do with your students. Suggestions for flipped classroom ideas are also included. Review the list of materials and additional resources, and prepare your lessons in advance. Using these activities in conjunction with your academic lessons will enable your students to gain a depth of understanding of grit and the social skills that promote it that only comes from practical application. The activities also create a positive, reinforcing environment where students can practice these skills. Coupled with Boys Town's social skills, this Activity Guide is a surefire way to give your students an opportunity to recognize and use grit in their daily lives.

SECTION 1

The old TV and movie Westerns portrayed a vivid picture of what we call "grit." Typically, the rugged, self-sufficient, brave, tough cowboy rolls into town and saves the day. He overcomes the elements and "bad guys" in order to persevere and succeed.

Most people know or have heard about people who seem to have so much ability but never seem to reach their potential for success. Then there are those individuals who don't possess as much natural ability but have achieved an unexplainable – sometimes, almost impossible – level of success. Furthermore, there are people who have persevered through life-altering disabilities in order to reach their goals.

So what makes some people fiercely strive to succeed while others remain mired in mediocrity? Winston Churchill shared a thought on this. He stated, "Continuous effort – not strength or intelligence – is the key to unlocking our true potential." In other words, the individual who succeeds or overcomes enormous obstacles is the one who possesses the most determination, the most perseverance, and most importantly, the most GRIT!

The purpose of the following lessons is to help students understand what grit is by exploring the vocabulary that surrounds the word, and the feelings and actions it can foster in people who possess it. Students must know what grit is before they can determine whether or not they possess it, and then pursue it.

This section includes the following activities:

- **G-R-I-T**
- **The Feeling of Grit**
- **The Shape of Grit**

G-R-I-T

OBJECTIVES

Social Skills: Students will practice following instructions and completing good quality work.

Executive Functions: Students will demonstrate the ability to work hard and complete an activity. They also will exercise self-control by beginning their work right away.

MATERIALS NEEDED

- Newspapers, magazines, and Internet sites where words that represent "grit" can be found
- Foam letters that spell G-R-I-T (letters also could be made from wood or another sturdy material). You can either have one large set of letters for your classroom or provide each student with a small set.

- Scissors
- Modge Pod or other decoupage glue
- Paint brushes
- Popsicle sticks
- Markers
- Visual of the social skill, "Following Instructions"
- Visual of the social skill, "Doing Good Quality Work"

DIRECTIONS

1. Before beginning this activity, cut out the foam letters that spell G-R-I-T (one classroom set or a set for each student). Make the letters large enough so students can later glue words and photos on them.

2. Remind the students about the steps of **"Following Instructions"** before starting:

    a. **Look at the teacher while instructions are being given.**

    b. **Say "Okay," or smile and nod your head.**

    c. **Do what you've been asked to do right away.**

3. Have the students search through newspapers, magazines, Internet sites, or other sources and find 20-25 examples (words, stories, phrases, quotes, or pictures) of grit.

4. Have students discuss their examples after you remind them about the steps of **"Doing Good Quality Work."**

   a. **After receiving the instructions, assemble the necessary materials and tools.**

   b. **Carefully begin working while focusing your attention on the task.**

   c. **Continue working until the task is completed.**

   d. **Examine your work, correct any deficiencies, and check back with the teacher.**

5. Have students cut out their word or picture examples of grit and decoupage them to the G-R-I-T letters.

6. Have students identify their favorite word pertaining to grit and have them copy it onto a Popsicle stick.

7. Put the Popsicle sticks in a container. Before a future task or a lengthy, difficult assignment, pull out a few of the Popsicle sticks and read the words on them to the class as a reminder to use grit in their schoolwork and their lives.

8. Display the foam G-R-I-T letters as a constant visual reminder of the value of perseverance, hard work, and not giving up when things get hard.

Show the students how to decoupage their grit examples onto the G-R-I-T letters.

The Feeling of Grit

OBJECTIVES

Social Skills: Students will develop the ability to persevere on a task or project.

Executive Functions: Students will display grit by finishing this project despite the difficulty of the task.

MATERIALS NEEDED

- *GRIT & Bear It!* book
- Newspapers, magazines
- Examples of redacted poems or writings
- Black markers, paint, or construction paper
- Scissors
- Paper
- Visual of the social skill, "Persevering on Tasks and Projects"

DIRECTIONS

1. Have students review the newspapers or magazines and select an article to use.

2. Explain to students what a redacted poem is and show examples.

3. Ask the students to write a message, rap song, or advertisement about grit on a piece of paper. The message can include a definition of grit, how to develop it, something inspirational about it, the price of it, or how to get it. You also can include your own ideas, depending on what you think your students need to know about grit.

4. Demonstrate for students how to circle the words in the articles they want to use and black out words they do not want in order to create a redacted version of their message, rap song, or advertisement (students can use black markers or paint).

5. Have students use markers or paint to create their redacted writings. Another option would be to have students cut out the words they want to use from construction paper and then paste the words on a colored piece of paper to construct their message.

6. Review the *GRIT & Bear It!* book with students. Discuss the importance of perseverance. Show students pages 18-19 and ask how long they think a mural of this nature would take to create.

7. Tell students this activity takes time and effort if it is to turn out right. Ask them to brainstorm techniques they will use to persevere on this project. After hearing several ideas and suggestions, share the following steps of the skill, **"Persevering on Tasks and Projects"**:

   a. **Know exactly what must be done. Be sure to ask questions if you are unsure.**

   b. **Get started right away.**

   c. **Remain on task even if it takes longer than expected to complete.**

   d. **Appropriately deal with frustrations or disappointments.** *(Remind students that they develop grit when they can overcome frustrations and keep working.)*

8. Have students display their redacted writings.

Practice making a redacted writing before starting this lesson. Encourage all students to try to find the words in articles in a way that brings a flare of creativity to the assignment. Some students may not be challenged by simply cutting out words and pasting them into their "writing."

Flipped Classroom: Post links to redacted types of writing on your website or blog. Ask each student to write down five tips they would give someone when performing this type of task. Have students share the tips in class the next day and then have them begin their own redacted writings.

Additional Resources: Search for information on "How to make a redacted poem" for a more complete and accurate method of construction.

The Shape of Grit

Social Skills: Students will follow instructions and work independently at producing good quality work.

Executive Functions: While following instructions, students will work independently with focus.

MATERIALS NEEDED

- *GRIT & Bear It!* book
- Examples of "shape poetry"
- Internet access to Tagxedo or Wordle
- Paper
- Pencils
- Colors/Markers
- Visual of the social skill, "Doing Good Quality Work"

Self-expression through poetry may be very difficult for some students to do. Encouraging them to stick with it and to keep trying will reinforce the concept of developing more grit in their lives.

DIRECTIONS

1. Review the *GRIT & Bear It!* book with students, highlighting various ways grit is demonstrated.

2. Show the students several examples of "shape poetry" (e.g., "concrete shape poetry" involves writing a poem in the shape of a particular object). Tagxedo and Wordle are a few online sources that show how to construct shape poetry.

3. Ask students to think of an animal, character, or object they feel would best represent the concept of "grit" and have them draw a picture of it. They shouldn't spend too much time on this drawing, but they should at least create an outline sketch. Use the following steps of the skill, **"Doing Good Quality Work,"** to remind students that it's important to follow all instructions carefully and to diligently work independently so they can produce high-quality work:

    a. After receiving the instructions, assemble the necessary materials and tools.

    b. Carefully begin working while focusing your attention on the task.

    c. Continue working until the task is completed.

    d. Examine your work, correct any deficiencies, and check back with the teacher.

4. Have students focus on the object, animal, or character they drew earlier and have them write a poem about grit.

5. When students are finished with their poems, have them rewrite them in the shape of their object, animal, or character. It may take a few tries before they are able to achieve the look they want. Another option would be to have students section off their drawings with lines, write their poem in one section, and put single words or pictures that represent grit in the remaining sections. Have students color their shape poems. Remind them again of the importance of sticking with a task, which will help to develop more grit in their lives.

6. Post the shape poems in the classroom for others to see.

Showing students examples of what you are asking them to do will be invaluable. If you are using an on-line shape-generating site, be sure to try it yourself first to work out any glitches.

Flipped Classroom: Ask students to view Tagxedo, Wordle, and an example of concrete shape poetry online. Have them describe in writing which one they would like to use and why. Also, post several poetry formats on the class website or blog and ask students to pick the type of poetry they would like to write when they come to class.

Additional Resources: Set up free accounts on the poetry site and other sites that you choose to use. Have students log in using your log-in information or have them create their own free account. If you have them use your login, be sure to change your password after completing the activity.

SECTION 2

Got Grit?

Putting a name to the ability to overcome obstacles and persevere helps us to recognize the meaning of "grit," but how do we know if we possess it? There are simple ways for a person to assess whether or not he or she possesses grit. Discovering individual motivation and learning how to effectively set goals not only can help people assess the amount of grit they have in their lives, but also can help them develop more grit.

Acquiring grit gives individuals an advantage over others who do not possess this trait. People with the greatest amount of grit believe they can improve their lives through hard work and perseverance. They deliberately direct their energies and thoughts to succeeding. They keep going long after others have given up.

The following activities are included in this section:

- **What Motivates Me?**
- **Pull Yourself Up by Your Bootstraps**
- **Fist Pump**
- **Making Time Count**
- **Dominoes**

What Motivates Me?

MATERIALS NEEDED

- A very heavy object, like a full file cabinet, a pile of bricks or stones, etc.
- Some type of reward, such as free "No Homework" passes, gift cards, or food
- Paper
- Pencils
- "What Motivates Me?/What Makes Me Want to Give Up?" T-chart Worksheet
- Visual of the social skill, "Staying On Task"
- Visual of the social skill, "Waiting Your Turn"

Explain to students that they CAN learn and achieve their goals, but many times they may not be motivated to do so. They either won't have the motivation to begin with, or they'll try to delay gratification, causing them to give in or give up. Their motivation will wane and they'll lose hope. In fact, some students come to school already defeated – physically, mentally, or emotionally.

DIRECTIONS

1. Place a heavy object in the center or a designated area of the room.

2. Remind students of the steps of **"Waiting Your Turn"**:

    a. **Sit quietly, while waiting your turn, and remain still.**

    b. **Avoid begging, whining, or making other noises while waiting.**

    c. **Engage in the activity when asked to do so.**

    d. **Thank the person who gives you a turn.**

3. One at a time, have the students try to move the heavy object five feet without tipping it over. Do not say anything or encourage students at this point. Most students will not be able to move the object and will give up. Some will give up more quickly than others.

4. Ask the students why they could not move the object. Ask them if they really care about moving it. (Most students will say they don't really care if they can do it.)

5. Explain to the students that in order to succeed, they must stay on task, even when it is hard, and not give up. Go over the following steps of **"Staying On Task"** with the class:

    a. Look at the task or assignment.

    b. Think about the steps that are needed to complete the task.

    c. Focus all your attention on your task.

    d. Stop working on the task only if given permission by the adult who gave you the task, or if you reach your goal.

    e. Ignore distractions and interruptions by others.

6. Encourage the students to try to move the object again (one at a time). This time, offer a reward (free "No Homework" pass, etc.) for whoever can do it. Praise students who try again for their efforts. Give a reward of your choosing to students who move the object this time.

7. Discuss motivation with the students. Ask what made them want to work harder to accomplish the task the second time, and ask what makes them want to give up. Point out that there won't always be an external reward for accomplishing a task, and that some motivation has to come from within.

8. Give each student a "What Motivates Me?/What Makes Me Want to Give Up?" Worksheet. On the "What Motivates Me?" side, have them write a list of things that motivate them. Ask them to put a star by their top two motivators. Then, on the other side, have them write a list of obstacles that make them want to give up on their goals or work. Ask them to put a star by two obstacles they will work to overcome.

Note in your own records what motivates each student. This could be beneficial for future activities and tasks. Also, make sure students are safe and do not injure themselves while trying to move the object.

Flipped Classroom Ideas: Post a video clip on motivation on the class website or class blog. (There are numerous video clips on YouTube and other sites featuring athletes and other determined people.) Ask the students to watch the video clip and generate a list of things that motivate them and a list of obstacles that make them want to give up on their goals. Have them bring the lists to the next class.

Name: _____ Date: _____

What Motivates Me?
What Makes Me Want to Give Up?

DIRECTIONS: On the "What Motivates Me?" side, write a list of things that motivate you and put a star by your top two motivators. Then, on the other side, write a list of obstacles that make you want to give up on your goals or work, and put a star by two obstacles you will work to overcome.

What Motivates Me?

What Makes Me Want to Give Up?

Pull Yourself Up by Your Bootstraps

OBJECTIVES

Social Skills: Students will practice choosing appropriate words to say while responding to and writing grit quotes.

Executive Functions: Students will gain a better understanding of what it means to possess grit. Students will display curiosity in searching for deeper meanings in the grit quotes.

MATERIALS NEEDED

- Grit quotes
- Paper
- Pencils
- Access to computers

- Colored paper for mounting the grit quotes
- Visual of the social skill, "Choosing Appropriate Words to Say"

DIRECTIONS

1. Prior to class, find several quotes on grit, perseverance, or determination in books, on posters, or on the Internet. (Some examples are included at the end of this activity.)

2. Write the quotes on pieces of colored paper and post them around the room.

3. When the students arrive for class, have them read the quotes.

4. Have the students select three quotes they like and have them write a response to the author for each of the quotes. Have them include:

   a. What they think the quote or statement means

   b. Whether they agree or disagree with the author and why

   c. How this quote could change a life

5. Remind students of the importance of using appropriate and good word choices when they are writing their reactions to the quotes. Have them brainstorm adjectives and words they can use, and make a master list on chart paper or on a marker board. As they think about

the responses they are going to write, review with them the steps of the skill, **"Choosing Appropriate Words to Say"**:

 a.   **Know the meaning of the words you are going to use.**

 b.   **Avoid using words that would offend someone or would be confusing. Also refrain from using slang, profanity, or words with a sexual meaning.**

 c.   **Then, make a decision on the words to use and write them down.**

6.   Ask students to write one statement about grit. The statement should tell what grit is and how it could change someone's life.

7.   Have the students compose their own quote about grit and design a poster of the quote on the computer or create their own handmade poster. Then hang the posters around the classroom or school.

It is helpful to go over the students' word choices as you begin this lesson. Have the students examine the use of "colorful" adjectives in their writing. Explain how some words are better than others when conveying a message or the meaning of a statement.

Flipped Classroom: Post the students' quotes or statements on grit online and ask students to review them and come to class with their top three. Focus your attention in the classroom on having the students write their responses, make their word choices, and design their own quotes. You also could have the students find their own quotes on grit and bring those to class. Another possibility would be to post a lesson on word choices online for the students to view before coming to class. Then have them write down 8-10 words they could use on the topic of grit and perseverance.

Additional Resources: Word Choice Resources and Adjective Resources.

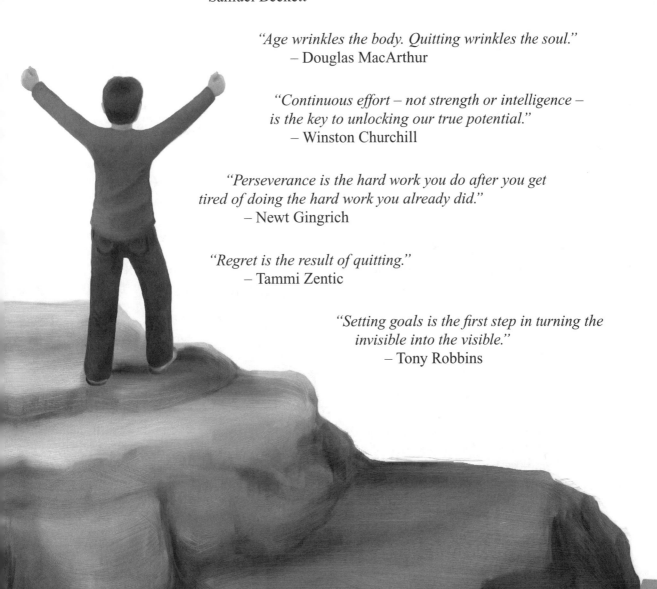

POSSIBLE QUOTES

"Pull yourself up by your bootstraps."
  – Sanford Renshaw

"Many of life's failures are people who do not realize how close they were to success when they gave up."
  – Thomas Edison

"Talent does not determine success, grit does."
  – Dillon Williams

"Ever tried. Ever failed. No matter. Try again. Fail again. Fail better."
  – Samuel Beckett

"Age wrinkles the body. Quitting wrinkles the soul."
  – Douglas MacArthur

"Continuous effort – not strength or intelligence – is the key to unlocking our true potential."
  – Winston Churchill

"Perseverance is the hard work you do after you get tired of doing the hard work you already did."
  – Newt Gingrich

"Regret is the result of quitting."
  – Tammi Zentic

"Setting goals is the first step in turning the invisible into the visible."
  – Tony Robbins

Fist Pump

Social Skills: Students will practice assessing their own abilities and setting goals based on those abilities.

Executive Functions: Students will be able to honestly assess the amount of grit they currently have.

MATERIALS NEEDED

- *GRIT & Bear It!* book
- Large piece of paper
- Markers
- "Grit Scale" Worksheet
- "Fist Grit" Worksheet
- Visual of the social skill, "Assessing Your Own Abilities"

DIRECTIONS

1. Review the *GRIT & Bear It!* book with students. Discuss the importance of having grit, referring to pages 12, 13, and 22.

2. Tell students they are going to be asked to honestly assess the amount of grit they believe they have in their lives at the present time. Review with students the steps of **"Assessing Your Own Abilities"**:

   a. **Make a list of your strengths and weaknesses.**

   b. **List situations in which you have been successful or have had problems.**

   c. **Plan future activities in consideration of your abilities.**

3. Ask students to use the following criteria when assessing themselves:

   a. Make a list of where you have grit in your life.

   b. List situations in which you have displayed grit.

   c. Identify how you could develop more grit and display it in future activities.

4. Hand out a "Grit Scale" Worksheet to each student. Have them complete the three criteria areas at the top and use their responses to determine their grit rating on a scale from 1 to 10, with 1 being the lowest and 10 being the highest. Then have them plot their own grit rating on the Grit Scale at the bottom. Make sure you compliment and encourage each student, regardless of his or her grit rating, and thank students for being honest.

5. Draw a line down the middle of the large piece of paper to create two columns. In the first column, write the heading, "Long-Term Goals," and list several goals students named during a previous activity. In the second column, write the heading, "Short-Term Goals." Have the students discuss the difference between a long-term goal and a short-term goal (short-term is soon; long-term is more than a year).

LONG-TERM GOALS

Examples should go here.

SHORT-TERM GOALS

Examples should go here.

6. Give each student a "Fist Grit" Worksheet. Ask students to write down a short-term goal that would help them display more grit in their lives (e.g., get an "A" on the next test) on the palm on the fist. Then have them write down at least four steps that will help them achieve that goal (e.g., study for one hour every night before the day of the test) on the fingers of the fist. Discuss the meaning of a fist pump or the act of raising one's fists as a sign of victory.

7. Display the students' "Fist Grit" Worksheets somewhere in the room at a lower eye level. When a student reaches his or her goal, move that student's fist up to a higher spot. This represents the fist being pumped in the air as a sign of victory.

(Optional) You could also use a paper shaped like a hand with the index finger extended, the symbol for saying "We're Number One!" In this case, have students write their short-term goal on the extended index finger and the four steps to achieving it across the other fingers' knuckles. Then have the students fold the index finger down. When they reach their goal, have them raise the index finger as if to say, "We're Number One!"

Students will produce more detailed steps for achieving their goal if you take the time to demonstrate an example for them. Be specific in the steps, telling the students that a specific plan of action will increase the likelihood that they will reach their goal.

Additional Resources: Goal-setting tips.

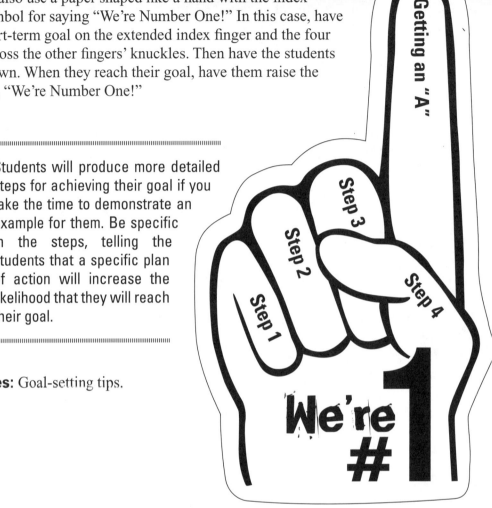

Name: _____ Date: _____

Grit Scale

Make a list of where you have grit in your life.	**List situations in which you have displayed grit.**	**Identify how you could develop more grit and display it in future activities.**
1._____ _____	_____ _____	_____ _____
2._____ _____	_____ _____	_____ _____
3._____ _____	_____ _____	_____ _____

Name: _____ Date: _____

Fist Grit

DIRECTIONS: Write down a short-term goal that would help you display more grit in your life on the palm on the fist. Then write down at least four steps that will help you achieve that goal on the fingers of the fist.

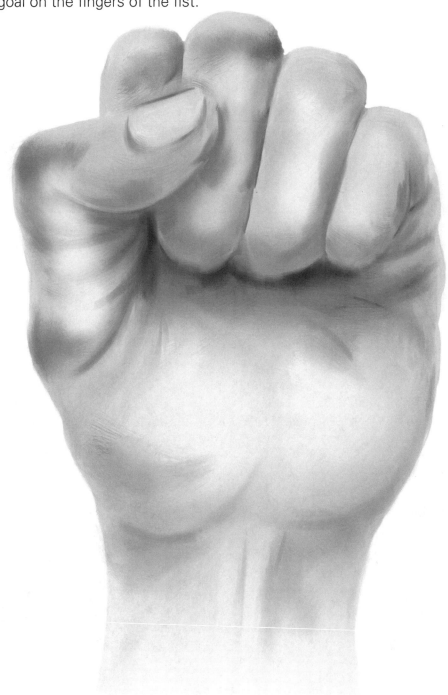

Making Time Count

Social Skills: Students will analyze, plan, and set a time frame for the steps (tasks) that need to be completed in order to achieve a class goal.

Executive Functions: Students will plan a series of steps for reaching a goal and will display an optimistic attitude when encountering frustrations or setbacks during the process.

MATERIALS NEEDED

- A class goal
- Timeline
- Paper
- Pencils
- Poster paper

- Colored pencils
- "Reach Your Goal" Handout
- Visual of the social skill, "Analyzing Tasks to Be Completed"

The importance of this activity is having students see the progress they make while working toward a class goal over the course of the school year or for a specified amount of time. This activity will provide a daily visual reminder of the goal and the steps being completed to successfully attain the desired outcome. The intent is to create a classroom environment of grit.

DIRECTIONS

1. Decide the goal you want the class to work toward. The goal could be having every student get a passing test score on a particular unit, or having everyone score well on a big standardized test at the end of the school year. It also could be something like having all the students turn their papers in on time, or achieving a character-focused goal (e.g., every student contributes to a food drive for a local pantry). As an example for this activity, we'll use the goal of having students score well on a CRT test at the end of a 12-week unit of study. Besides deciding on a goal, also decide on a reward the class will receive for achieving the goal (e.g., a class party).

2. Construct a timeline, giving thought to the number of tasks (steps) you want students to complete in order to reach the goal (e.g., a timeline could be a drawing of a football field on which a cutout person moves toward a goal line as tasks are completed until he reaches the end zone). Ten steps are about right because it gives students a good idea of the details they need to attend to while working toward their goal without seeming burdensome. The number of steps may change, depending on the goal that is selected and/or the age and ability of the students.

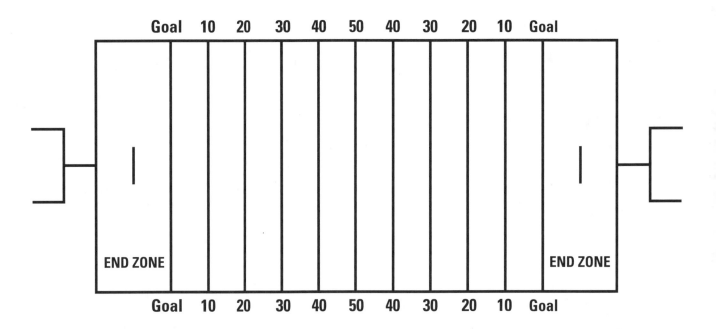

3. Tell the students what the class goal is and what the reward will be if they achieve it in the set time frame. Have them use the skill of **"Analyzing Tasks to Be Completed"** to brainstorm and analyze ideas for the steps they might need to take in order to achieve the goal. These skill steps are:

   a. **Clarify the goal.**

   b. **List the steps needed to achieve that goal and what will be required to accomplish each step.**

   c. **Put the steps in order.**

   d. **Write down all suggestions (be sure to include your own ideas).**

4. Condense the suggestions into the top 10 steps students will need to take to reach the goal. Set a time frame for each step.

5. Divide the class into 10 groups. Give each group one step and have group members make a poster with the information and completion date for their step. They can illustrate the poster if they want. Have each group hang its poster at the spot on the class goal timeline that depicts its step and completion date.

6. Update the timeline every time a step is achieved. **If the step is not achieved within the set time frame, have students continue their work on the step but discuss what has to happen. Remind students that it might require them to plan ahead, revise some of the other steps, or reset completion dates. The important thing for students to realize is that even though they may encounter setbacks and frustrations that could change the original plan, they need to DISPLAY GRIT, KEEP GOING, and KEEP WORKING toward the class goal.**

7. Once the goal is reached, celebrate and give the reward.

Set a class goal that will benefit your students. Make sure you really celebrate when the students reach their goal. Reinforce the concept of grit. **If for some reason the class does not reach its goal, emphasize the importance of the effort they made. This teaches the lesson that even though we may not always meet our goals in the way we expect, we can and should always give it our best effort!**

Additional Resources: A list of possible goals you feel the class might want to meet.

Dominoes

Social Skills: Students will set a goal and plan the steps necessary to achieve it.

Executive Functions: Students will display goal-directed persistence in planning the steps necessary to achieve their goal.

MATERIALS NEEDED

- Information on marathons
- Large piece of paper
- One domino for each student (could be a real domino, or pieces of wood or another material of domino size)
- "Plan of Action" Worksheet
- Paints or markers
- Paper
- Pencils
- Visual of the social skill, "Setting Goals"

DIRECTIONS

1. Before class begins, set up two domino "tracks" (stand up a number of dominoes in a line so that when you tip over the first one, it starts a chain reaction of falling dominoes). In the first track, leave a few gaps between dominoes so that when you tip over the first one, the chain reaction will stop when it reaches the gaps and not all the dominoes will fall. In the second track, keep the dominoes very close together so when you tip the first one, the chain reaction knocks down all the other dominoes.

2. Have students research marathons. Provide books or computer sites where they can find information on famous marathons, how to train for them, and how grit is involved. Have the students share the information they found while you write the information on a large piece of paper.

3. Ask students how their lives are like a marathon. Answers could include that we have just so many years to live and we must keep running, meeting goals along the way, or the better we train for life, the better race we run.

4. Relate this analogy to setting goals. Tell students that setting and achieving goals in life is more like a marathon than a sprint. While we do have some "sprint-type" goals, called short-term goals, most of our goals in life are long-term, like "marathons."

5. Go to the domino tracks you set up before class and use them to demonstrate to the students how achieving long-term goals requires many smaller steps along the way. Tell the students that if they don't take the time to set smaller goals as part of their long-term goal, they probably won't achieve it. Then tip the first domino of the first track (where there are gaps between the dominoes), and explain how the dominoes won't all fall down (the goal) because there are "steps" (the gaps) missing. Then go to the second track and tip the first domino. This time, all the dominos should fall down. Explain to the students that when we set up our goals step by step, we are more likely to achieve them.

6. Hand out a "Plan of Action" Worksheet to each student. Give them time to think of a goal and have them write a plan for reaching it on the handout. Encourage the students to come up with a long-term goal that has multiple steps. Before they start, explain the five steps to the skill of **"Setting Goals."**

   a. **"Dream It."** Decide on your goal. Set high goals, and think about your values and desires.

   b. **"Plan It."** Write down the sequence of steps needed to achieve the goal. List any resources you will need.

   c. **"Work It."** Write out a "working" plan. Examine each step and allow time for steps that may take longer or require more work.

   d. **"Endure It."** Write down what you will do if you get frustrated or experience a setback or an obstacle. Remain flexible so you can adapt your steps to changing circumstances.

   e. **"Own It."** Write down the date you will "own" your goal, and what emotions you think you will have.

7. Finally, give each student a domino and encourage them to decorate it with something that will help them keep going when they face frustrations or difficulties in trying to reach their goals.

Make a list of categories of topics students can choose a goal from (athletics, academics, self-improvement, peer relations, interaction or communication with others, etc.).

Flipped Classroom: Post links and videos on marathons for the students to view. Ask them to answer the questions about marathons and decide on their goal before coming to class.

Additional Resources: Have websites available where students can research marathons in case they have difficulty locating their own. Provide goal-setting links.

Name: _____ Date: _____

Plan of Action

DIRECTIONS: Use the following steps to help you make a plan for setting and "owning" your goal.

....

DREAM IT

Values and desires needed to own a goal

> _____

_____

....

PLAN IT

Sequence of steps and resources needed to achieve the goal

> _____

_____

....

WORK IT

The working plan of the steps needed

> _____

_____

....

ENDURE IT

Plans for overcoming frustrations, obstacles, and setbacks

> _____

_____

....

OWN IT

Date goal is to be completed and the emotions you think you will have

> _____

_____

....

SECTION  3

Our Heritage

The pride of America is in our entrepreneurial, opportunistic mindset. Immigrants flock to the United States because our nation was founded on the idea that ALL people can achieve their dreams and goals with hard work and perseverance. America has been a beacon of hope for many.

The stories of those who have triumphed inspire us. When we hear of individuals overcoming difficult obstacles and odds, it makes us want to try harder and be better. The following activities are meant to inspire your students and provide examples of how grit has afforded success to many. The lessons also are meant to serve as a guide for students in developing their own grit by learning from the stories of those individuals we find not only in our own communities but also across this great country of ours.

The following activities are included in this section:

- **Red, White, & Blue**
- **Finding Grit**
- **Overcomer**
- **Ask the Expert/Grit Testimony**
- **Does the Past Live On?**

Red, White, & Blue

OBJECTIVES

Social Skills: Students will follow the steps of contributing to discussions and talking with others.

Executive Functions: Students will be able to identify grit and set goals to develop their own grit. By actively participating, students will demonstrate zest for their schoolwork as well as our country.

MATERIALS NEEDED

- *GRIT & Bear It!* book
- Research (done in advance) on the history of pioneers, our Founding Fathers, and Labor Day
- "Flag" Worksheets
- Pencils
- Markers
- Visual of the social skills, "Contributing to Discussions/Talking with Others"

Explain to students that our country was built on hard work and grit, and it continues to be. The harder you work, the more opportunities you have for rewards. We celebrate a national holiday dedicated to the workers of America. It is called Labor Day. Many flags are flown on this day in tribute to the contributions workers have made to our country.

DIRECTIONS

1. Before beginning this activity, review with the students the importance and steps of the skills, **"Contributing to Discussions/Talking with Others."**

   a. **Look at the person who is talking.**

   b. **Wait for a time when nobody else is talking (avoid interrupting).**

   c. **Use a pleasant voice.**

   d. **Choose words that are not offensive or confusing.**

   e. **Make a short, appropriate comment that is related to the topic, or ask questions.**

   f. **Allow others to speak.**

2. Review the *GRIT & Bear It!* book with students.

3. Lead a discussion about our Founding Fathers and how they displayed grit.

4. Talk about how the early pioneers displayed grit.

5. Ask students what Labor Day is and why workers and students get this day off. After discussing this, share websites with students about Labor Day. Students will learn that Labor Day is a day dedicated to the social and economic achievements of American workers. It is a tribute to the contributions the workers have made to the strength, prosperity, and well-being of our country. Some suggested websites on the history of Labor Day are www.history.com/topics/labor-day and www.dol.gov/laborday/history.htm.

6. (Optional) To extend the discussions, ask more questions about the information students found on the websites.

7. After a discussion on the history of Labor Day, ask students how people display grit in their work today. Then ask them how their parents and people they know display grit at their jobs.

8. Ask students how they display grit in their work at school, in activities, or at home.

9. Show students pages 20-21 in the *GRIT & Bear It!* book.

10. Give each student a "Flag" Worksheet and ask them to draw an American flag in the box. Ask students to think of one area where they could set a specific goal to develop their grit and write that idea in the flag. Then have them write down the steps they can take to become "grittier" in the spaces below the flag. Have students color their flags.

11. Display the worksheets around the room.

Flipped Classroom: Ask students to view the websites that describe the history of Labor Day. Have them come to class with five facts they learned about Labor Day, including the founder's name and the first day it was recognized. During class time, discuss the holiday and do the "Flag" Worksheet activity, really focusing on helping the students to identify specific ways they could work toward attaining more grit in their lives.

Additional Resources: Explore other groups of people throughout history who displayed grit and resources that describe this. You also could invite workers from various industries in the community to come in and talk about how grit is involved in their work.

Name: _____ Date: _____

Flag

DIRECTIONS: Draw an American flag in the box. Think of one area where you could set a specific goal to develop your grit and write that idea in the flag. Write down the steps you can take to become "grittier" in the spaces below the flag. Then color your flag.

Steps to become "grittier"

1. _____

2. _____

3. _____

4. _____

Finding Grit

Social Skills: Students will apply their knowledge of grit or perseverance, and analyze tasks to be completed in order to create a presentation.

Executive Functions: Students will be able to identify grit as it is demonstrated by other people.

MATERIALS NEEDED

- Camera
- Access to Photoshop or www.photoshop.com (free version)
- Paper
- Pencils
- Internet access
- Visual of the social skill, "Task Analysis"

DIRECTIONS

1. Explain to the students that they will have two options in this activity.

   Option 1: Take pictures of people displaying grit and turn them into a presentation using Photoshop or another online presentation site.

   Option 2: Write about where they see grit and use that information to create a presentation.

2. Ask each student to choose an option and to analyze the tasks he or she will need to complete for the presentation. Have them write down their analysis and turn it into you before they begin. Remind them to use the steps of the skill, **"Task Analysis"**:

   a. **Clarify what the task or assignment is.**

   b. **List every step.**

   c. **Identify the steps in order.**

   d. **Make a plan to begin.**

3. Provide an overview (described in steps 4-7) of what the student presentations need to include. Explain the steps in a way that will make the most sense to your students.

4. Students must find 5 to 7 examples of where they see grit. It could be at school, at home, or somewhere in the community. Once they find an example, they either should write down a description of the entire situation where someone is displaying grit or take a photo of the example. (If they are taking a picture, students must ask the subject for permission to take the photo and use it in the class assignment.)

5. Students should place their written or photo examples in a web format.

6. After they make a web presentation of their examples, have the students go to the free Glogster Edu site. Here, they can create online posters or portraits of their grit examples. Another option would be to have students download their photos to the free site, www.photoshop.com. Here, students can edit and caption each photo and develop an online Power Point presentation.

7. When all the presentations are completed, use www.photoshop.com to compile all of them into a class presentation about where grit can be found in the school and community.

Visit and explore www.photoshop.com prior to the activity so you can tell students how to use the site. It also would be beneficial to walk students through the process of uploading a photo and captioning it.

Flipped Classroom: Have students post links to examples of individuals who are displaying grit to the class website or blog. Use these sites the next day to start the activity.

Additional Resources: Demonstrate how to use Photoshop.

Overcomer

OBJECTIVES

Social Skills: Students will recognize and identify how to alter one's environment to improve a situation.

Executive Functions: Students will identify how people try very hard, even after experiencing failure, and overcome setbacks. They will synthesize this information into their own tips for overcoming obstacles and persevering to achieve success.

MATERIALS NEEDED

- *GRIT & Bear It!* book
- Free version of the QR reader, downloaded on phones or iPads (see instructions under "Resources" at the end of this activity)
- "How to Be an Overcomer" flipchart or poster
- QR codes (instructions are at the end of this activity)

- Internet access
- Pencils
- "Video/Article" Worksheet (five copies for each group or student)
- Application questions
- "Tips to Overcoming Challenges" Worksheet
- Visual of the social skill, "Altering One's Environment"

DIRECTIONS

Prior to Class:

1. Do an Internet search and locate several websites or articles that focus on how an individual overcame overwhelming odds or disabilities in order to achieve success (e.g., Holocaust survivors; Derek Redmond, an athlete at the 1992 Olympic Games in Barcelona; Helen Keller, etc.). Be sure to choose several options that cover a variety of challenging situations.

2. Create a QR code for each website, write each code on a piece of paper, and display the papers around the room (only create QR codes for articles that can be found online).

3. Create a flipchart or poster with the title "How to Be an Overcomer" that students can write on.

4. Have students download the free version of the QR reader on their phones or iPads. If some students don't have a phone or iPad, have the class work in groups.

During Class:

5. To begin the activity, introduce students to the skill of **"Altering One's Environment"**:

    a. **Identify situations in which you encounter difficulty.**

    b. **Look for parts of those situations that could be changed to bring about improvement.**

    c. **Make appropriate changes to improve self-esteem, behavior, or performance.**

6. Review the *GRIT & Bear It!* book with students. Highlight the challenges overcome by the featured characters, focusing on page 23.

7. Tell students they are going to review qualities that some people have that make it easier for them to overcome obstacles or challenges, and succeed even when things become very difficult. Ask the students to think of a time when something was very hard for them, but they triumphed anyway. If they can't think of anything they have done, ask them to think of someone who has faced a difficult situation, but somehow managed to deal with it and overcome the difficulty. Instruct the students to write about their experience or the experience of the other person, reminding them to describe the obstacle and how it was overcome.

8. Have students capture the QR codes that are placed around the room on their mobile devices and view a total of five videos and/or articles at their desk or designated spot.

9. Distribute the "Video/Article" Worksheet to students (or post the questions from the worksheet on the board).

10. Ask students to answer the set of questions from the worksheet for each video/article they viewed:

    a. Which person persevered through his or her obstacle?

    b. What was the obstacle of difficulty?

    c. What did the person do when things got really tough?

    d. Is he or she different from people you know?

    e. What made him or her successful?

    f. How did he or she alter the environment?

    g. What lessons could we learn from this person?

11. Once the students have answered the worksheet questions for their five videos/articles, have them answer the following questions:

    a. How do people find the grit to overcome some of their challenges?

    b. Does how a person is raised have anything to do with it?

    c. What makes some people stronger (in terms of overcoming difficulties) than others?

    d. Does it help to have a good attitude (optimism)?

12. Discuss the answers students give as a class and write the answers on the "How to Be an Overcomer" poster.

13. Finally, hand out the blank "Tips to Overcoming Challenges" Worksheet and have students write five tips for overcoming obstacles and persevering to success they can share with others. Post the tip sheets on the "Overcomer" poster.

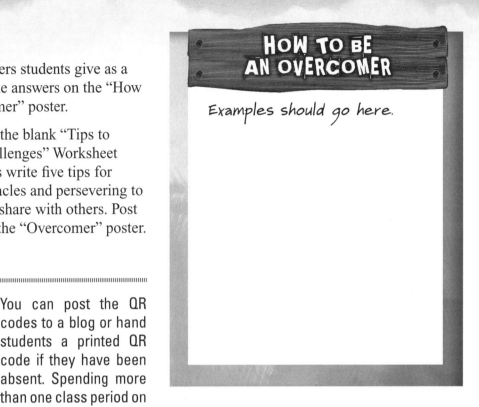

HOW TO BE AN OVERCOMER

Examples should go here.

You can post the QR codes to a blog or hand students a printed QR code if they have been absent. Spending more than one class period on this activity will help students better internalize the lessons that can be learned through examples of overcoming adversity.

Flipped Classroom: Post links to videos and articles on a class website or blog. Ask students to view five videos/articles and answer the worksheet questions for each one. Instruct students to bring the answers to class the next day. In class, ask each student to write about a time when he or she overcame a difficulty. Discuss the videos/articles, and then continue on with the remainder of the activity.

Additional Resources: After you have downloaded the QR reader app to your phone or iPad, you can start to make QR codes. Find a video or website you want the students to view and copy the website address. Then go to the QR reader. Under the "Creator" tab, you should see a "+" symbol. A dropdown will come up and give you choices of what to create. For copying a website, choose the "WebURL." Then paste in your URL address and press "Create." The address will now be under your "Creator" tab. You can then share or print off the website's QR code to display in the classroom.

Name: _____ Date: _____

Video/Article

DIRECTIONS: Answer the questions below about the person you researched.

1. Which person persevered through his or her obstacle? _____

    _____

    _____

2. What was the obstacle of difficulty?_____

    _____

3. What did the person do when things got really tough?_____

    _____

    _____

4. Is he or she different from people you know?_____

    _____

5. What made him or her successful?_____

    _____

    _____

6. How did he or she alter the environment? _____

    _____

7. What lessons could we learn from this person?_____

    _____

Name: _____ Date: _____

Tips to Overcoming Challenges

DIRECTIONS: Write five tips for overcoming obstacles and persevering to success you can share with others.

Ask the Expert/Grit Testimony

OBJECTIVES

Social Skills: Students will hear how others have persevered and will practice the skill of "Listening to Others."

Executive Functions: Students will recognize grit in others. Students will show self-control by allowing others to speak without interruption.

MATERIALS NEEDED

- Guest speaker
- Paper
- Pencils
- "What Did I Hear?" Worksheet

- Microphone, if needed
- Forms for captions
- Visual of the social skill, "Listening to Others"

DIRECTIONS

1. Line up a guest speaker or guest celebrity who can share how perseverance/grit made a difference in his or her life. (Pick someone who can talk about overcoming trials and persevering through hardships. It will have more impact if the students recognize who this person is.) Make sure the speaker knows he or she will be talking about having grit.

2. Prior to the guest speaker's appearance, tell the students a little about this person. Avoid sharing too much; provide just enough to spark their interest. Ask them to think of two questions they could ask this person.

3. Remind students of the appropriate way to listen to a guest speaker (**"Listening to Others"**):

   a. **Look at the person.**

   b. **Sit or stand quietly and refrain from fidgeting or giggling.**

   c. **Wait until the speaker has finished before you ask questions.**

   d. **Show you understand by nodding your head or by telling the speaker you appreciate him or her being there.**

4. Have the guest speaker talk with the students. Leave time for questions and answers. (Having the speaker talk before a very difficult test or project could serve as extra motivation!) While the speaker is presenting, take a photo you can print for use at the end of the activity.

5. Have the students ask the speaker their questions or follow-up questions.

6. Thank the speaker for coming.

7. After the speaker leaves, have the students complete the "What Did I Hear?" Worksheet.

8. Finally, ask students as a group to come up with a caption for the photo you took of the speaker, including something they learned about grit. Post the photo and the caption in the classroom as a visual reminder of how someone perseveres through difficulty.

Have your iPad or digital camera ready to take a photo on the day of the presentation. Prepare some background information on your speaker. If the speaker is well-known, ask the students to give you some information.

Name: _____ Date: _____

What Did I Hear?

1. List three facts you learned from the guest speaker.

   1) _____

   _____

   2) _____

   _____

   3) _____

2. In detail, list one take away from the presentation that will help you in the future.

   _____

   _____

   _____

3. Was the speaker beneficial to you? If so, how? If not, why?

   _____

   _____

   _____

   _____

4. What other questions do you have?

   _____

   _____

   _____

   _____

Does the Past Live On?

Teacher Note: This activity may be difficult for students who are separated from their parents or natural families, or who do not know their family history. Be sensitive when giving instructions, and adapt the activity for students as needed to "role model" grit where appropriate.

OBJECTIVES

Social Skills: Students will practice choosing appropriate words to say while writing letters/articles about a role model who displayed grit.

Executive Functions: Students will explore the ways their role models have displayed grit and what impact this has had on their lives.

MATERIALS NEEDED

- "Model of Grit" Worksheet
- Paper
- Pencils
- Colored pencils or other drawing supplies

Explain to students that cultural identity is a priceless gift, especially if it is given as part of honorable character. A person's family history shapes an individual's personality and behavior, which will continue to be passed down from one generation to the next. Displaying grit in our families can have long-lasting, positive effects.

DIRECTIONS

1. Tell students they are going to explore the pattern of grit in their own families or close circle of friends.

2. Have students think of a relative or role model who they feel displays or has displayed grit in his or her life.

3. Have students complete the "Model of Grit" Worksheet.

4. Ask students to draw a picture of the person they selected.

5. Have students share their answers to the following questions from the "Model of Grit" Worksheet:

    a. How did your relative/role model show grit?

    b. Was there a pattern of grit in his or her life?

    c. How did this person's grit impact you or your family?

    d. What lessons can you learn from him or her?

    e. How could you carry on this trait?

    f. Do you display this trait in your own life? If so, why do you think that, and if not, why do you think that is?

6. Have students write a letter to their role model (if living) or write an article about this person (if deceased) that thanks him or her for living out the quality of grit and describes how it has made a difference to the student. Encourage students to also write about how they could continue to pass on grit to the next generation.

Be sensitive to students who are separated from their family or who may not know their family history. If students do not know their relatives well enough, encourage them to think of some other person they know who displays grit.

Additional Resources: Examples of people who have displayed grit in their lives and how it impacted their families and other individuals around them

Name: _____ Date: _____

Model of Grit

1. How did your relative/role model show grit? _____

   _____

   _____

2. Was there a pattern of grit in his or her life? _____

   _____

3. How did this person's grit impact you or your family? _____

   _____

   _____

4. What lessons can you learn from him or her?_____

   _____

   _____

5. How could you carry on this trait?_____

   _____

   _____

6. Do you display this trait in your own life? If so, why do you think that, and if not,

   why do you think that is? _____

   _____

   _____

SECTION 4

Delaying the Reward

We live in a fast-paced, instant gratification-type of world. We rarely have to wait for anything in this day and age. News, music, communication, and entertainment are all just a click away. As convenient as this can be, is having all these things at our fingertips the best thing for the character development of an individual? Does instant gratification afford us the ability to develop those qualities that will help us endure the hardships of life?

The ability to overcome obstacles and endure hardships of many kinds, while delaying rewards, is what helps us meet the challenges of everyday life. Helping our young people develop a "gritty" character should be a top priority. Being able to delay gratification will enable young people to develop a dedicated, relentless drive that will help them overcome failures and endure setbacks.

The following activities are included in this section:

- **Now or Later?**
- **I Will Carry On**
- **Can YOU Do It?**
- **If – Then**

Now or Later?

Social Skills: Students will gain a better understanding of what delaying gratification means.

Executive Functions: Students will exhibit self-control and grit by learning to delay gratification.

MATERIALS NEEDED

- *GRIT & Bear It!* book
- Some type of candy or treat (be certain to comply with your school's or district's policy)
- Paper
- Pencils
- Various math problems to complete
- Visual of the social skill, "Delaying Gratification"

Explain to the students that you want them to have the ability to persevere through school, difficulties, and obstacles. Developing a "gritty" character is of utmost importance in our fast-paced, competitive world. Being able to delay gratification for work the students perform will help them develop a dedicated, relentless work ethic, which will help them overcome failures and setbacks throughout their lives.

DIRECTIONS

1. Ask students to complete one minute's worth of math problems.

2. When they've finished, tell the students they may have one treat because they finished one minute's worth of math problems. Then let them know they could have three treats if they complete three more minutes of math problems. (You can change the time and number of treats best fit your students' abilities.)

3. After the students have made their choices, completed any extra math problems, and received their treats, have them discuss why some students wanted their treats right away and others were willing to work for three more minutes in order to get more. Explain what delaying gratification is and how working longer for a better reward that comes later is a good example.

4. Review the *Grit & Bear it!* book with the class. Draw attention to page 26, and ask the class if they've ever been part of a competitive tournament. Explain that in a tournament, even if you win many games, you don't always win the trophy. And when you do, it's usually only after several days of working hard. This is an example of delayed gratification.

5. Ask the students to imagine that everyone in the class was going to try to delay gratification with the math problems and treats. Ask them what strategies they would use. Have the students come up with several ideas and then share with them the following steps for the skill of **"Delaying Gratification"**:

    a. **Identify the want.**

    b. **Tell yourself you can wait for what you want (e.g., candy).**

    c. **Remain calm and relaxed.**

    d. **Find ways or activities to focus your attention. Avoid thinking about getting the reward or payoff right away.**

6. Ask the students to make a list of the benefits of delaying gratification on a piece of paper. Have them write down what would have made them want to delay their gratification in this particular activity.

Check for student food allergies before giving out the candy or treats. Make the first set of math problems difficult so students will be tempted to not delay gratification.

Flipped Classroom: On your class website or blog, post videos or lectures on the definition and the benefits of delaying gratification. Quiz students on this concept when they come to class.

I Will Carry On

OBJECTIVES

Social Skills: Students will adopt and practice a new good habit that displays grit over a period of time, and will delay gratification for a set period of time. Students will exercise the privilege of rewarding themselves.

Executive Functions: Students will display persistence in attaining their new good habit, even if they experience some degree of failure.

MATERIALS NEEDED

- *GRIT & Bear It!* book
- "Hand & Torch" Worksheet
- Olympic torch information
- Paper

- Pencils
- Visual of the social skill, "Rewarding Yourself"

Explain to the students that the Olympic torch has been a symbol of the Olympic Games since the Games began in ancient Greece. In 1936, the torch tradition was broadened with the start of a torch relay that begins in Olympia (symbolic of the ancient Games) and ends at the site of the Olympics. The torch's flame then stays lit until the closing ceremony of the Olympics. The torch is a symbol of "Carrying On" the tradition. It takes grit, determination, and perseverance to run in the torch relay for each Olympics. In the same way, grit, determination, and perseverance are the foundational blocks for Olympic athletes.

DIRECTIONS

1. Hold a class discussion on the Olympics. See what the students already know, and add in any information that you choose.

2. Ask students how difficult they think it is to become an Olympic athlete. What does it take? Would being an Olympic athlete take dedication? Would it take perseverance? Why? Would it take grit? In what ways? Ask students to write their answers to these questions on a piece of paper.

3. Ask the students if they think these athletes would have to set several goals along the way to achieve their high level of success. Discuss how they would set short-term, mid-term, and long-term goals along the way to making it to the Olympics. Then ask the students if the athletes would have to do anything else (e.g., raise money, overcome injuries, etc.).

4. Give students 90 seconds to think about the differences between a good habit and a bad habit. Have students share their thoughts. Explain to the students that the general thinking is that it takes approximately 21 days to form a habit, whether it is a good one or a bad one. So if students do something for 21 days straight, it should become a new habit. Ask the students to think of habits Olympic athletes would have to form in order to be successful. (These might include eating a well-balanced diet, getting plenty of sleep, training a certain number of hours a day, etc.)

5. Have each student select a goal he or she would like to accomplish 21 days from now. Hand out the "Hand & Torch" Worksheet and have the students write their goal on the flame part. Then ask them to write one habit they will have to form in order to attain their goal on the handle part of the torch. (For example, if a student wants to score 90% or better on the next science test, she must get into the habit of reviewing her class notes and science book for 10 minutes every evening.)

6. Ask students to pick a reward they will give themselves when they reach their goal. Have them write this on the back of the torch.

7. Have each student select an "accountability buddy" who will ask him or her at the end of each week if he or she practiced the good habit every day. Stress the importance of being honest on this activity.

8. At the end of the 21 days, have the students reward themselves if they practiced their habit for all 21 days, even if they did not reach their goal (just as Olympic athletes can reward themselves even if they do not win a gold medal). Tell the students to follow these steps when using the skill of **"Rewarding Yourself"**:

   a. **Decide if what you did was praiseworthy.**

   b. **If so, tell yourself that and feel good about it.**

   c. **Give yourself an extra privilege or reward.**

   d. **Prompt yourself to increase your competency and ability.**

Do research on an Olympic athlete to see what specific habits he or she formed in order to help the students develop their goals and habits.

Flipped Classroom: Post information and links about the Olympic torch. Ask the students to review the information and come to class the next day with a summary of the history of the Olympic torch and the Olympic torch relay, and what significance they hold for the Olympics.

Additional Resources: Find a video or YouTube video of the Olympic torch relay.

Name: _____ Date: _____

Hand & Torch

DIRECTIONS: Write the goal you want to accomplish 21 days from now on the flame part of the torch. Then, on the handle part of the torch, write one habit you will have to form in order to attain your goal. On the back of the torch, write a reward you will give yourself for reaching your goal.

Can YOU Do It?

Social Skills: Students will display effort as they perform tasks and will gain an understanding of the advantages of delaying gratification.

Executive Functions: Students will display grit by continuing to work at accomplishing tasks, even after experiencing failure.

MATERIALS NEEDED

- 3 golf balls
- A challenging jigsaw/crossword/ word search puzzle
- Several difficult story problems

- Paper
- Pencils
- Visual of the social skill, "Displaying Effort"

DIRECTIONS

1. Prior to the activity, set up stations where students will work on the challenging tasks.

2. Explain each station to the students. At Station 1, have the students try to stack the three golf balls in a tower. The tower must stay up for at least 10 seconds without falling over. Station 2 should have a challenging jigsaw, crossword, or word search puzzle(s) for the students to put together or solve. Station 3 should have several difficult story problems to solve.

3. Tell the students they can choose to do one, two, or all three of the activities. When they complete an activity, students must get your approval before moving on to the next one.

   Explain the following rewards:

   - If a student chooses to do one activity and completes it successfully, he or she will receive 20 minutes of free computer time (or another reward of his or her choice).
   - If a student completes two activities successfully, he or she will receive 30 minutes of free computer time and can invite a friend to eat lunch with him or her in the classroom.
   - If a student diligently completes all three activities successfully, he or she will receive 30 minutes of free computer time, lunch with a friend, and a free "No Homework" pass. (You can change these rewards based on your students.)

4. Tell students that it will take some effort to complete the tasks, so they will need to follow the steps of **"Displaying Effort"**:

   a. **Remain on task and work diligently.**

   b. **Do your best.**

   c. **Remember to inform the teacher before you move on to a new task.**

5. Take some class time to explain the stations, but have the students work on the tasks during their free time. This will help demonstrate who has perseverance a little more clearly. After giving the students what you feel is ample time to work on the tasks, see where the students stand.

6. Discuss with the students why they chose to try to complete the number of tasks they did, and reward each student accordingly. If a student chose only one activity, ask why he or she did not try for another one. If a student completed all three tasks, have him or her explain what drove him or her to persevere. Point out that completing all three activities showed grit and delayed gratification.

7. Have the students write answers to the following question on a piece of paper: "Would you prefer to receive $1 million today, or take a penny today and double it every day for a month and then take that amount after 31 days?" Collect the answers and tally them as a class. (Taking the penny adds up to more than $1 million.)

8. Ask the students to do the math and figure out how much money a penny doubled every day for a month would total.

9. Point out that sometimes we take what we feel is a good reward because it is easier, when often we can earn an even better reward if we work a little harder and wait a little longer.

Make sure all the puzzles are age-appropriate for your students.

59

If – Then

OBJECTIVES

Social Skills: Students will gain a better understanding of how to apply delayed gratification to their lives.

Executive Functions: Students will work independently, with focus, to gain a better understanding of delayed gratification.

MATERIALS NEEDED

- Paper
- Pencils
- "Interview Questions" Worksheet
- Visual of the social skill, "Delaying Gratification"

DIRECTIONS

1. Remind students of the meaning and the steps of the skill, **"Delaying Gratification."** The steps are:

    a. **Identify the want.**

    b. **Tell yourself you can wait for what you want (e.g., candy).**

    c. **Remain calm and relaxed.**

    d. **Find ways or activities to focus your attention. Avoid thinking about getting the reward or payoff right away.**

2. Demonstrate an "If – Then" statement for the students. Discuss the meaning of "inference" (drawing conclusions from what you already know).

3. Ask students to practice writing five to ten "If – Then" statements. The statements should focus on delaying gratification or waiting for something better. (For example: "If I finish studying one chapter by five o'clock, then I can play a video game for 20 minutes.")

4. For homework, ask the students to interview two people about delaying gratification. Have them use the following questions from the "Interview Questions" Worksheet as a guide:

    a. What does delaying gratification mean to you?

    b. Have you ever used delaying gratification in your life? If so, was it worth the wait?

    c. What advice would you give others about delaying gratification?

    d. Can you think of an "If – Then" statement about delaying gratification to share?

5. Have students bring the answers to their interview questions back to class and share them as a group.

6. When all the statements have been presented, have students pick the Top Ten "If – Then" statements and discuss their meanings. Then post them in the classroom.

Have a few "If – Then" statements prepared in advance to use as a guide for students who might struggle with this activity.

Additional Resources: Provide visual examples of "If – Then" statements.

Name: _____ Date: _____

Interview Questions

1. What does delaying gratification mean to you?

   _____

   _____

   _____

   _____

2. Have you ever used delaying gratification in your life? If so, was it worth the wait?

   _____

   _____

   _____

   _____

3. What advice would you give others about delaying gratification?

   _____

   _____

   _____

   _____

4. Can you think of an "If – Then" statement about delaying gratification to share?

   _____

   _____

   _____

   _____

SECTION 5

Handling the 'Oops' of Life

It is human nature to make mistakes. The average person will make many of them throughout his or her life. Some will be minor and others will be major. What is important is that we learn from our mistakes so we know what to do in future situations.

At times, we have a double standard for students when it comes to mistakes. On one hand, we want them to excel in the classroom without any problems. Yet, we tell them to take risks and be creative. There are set answers to certain problems, but we sometimes encourage students to analyze these problems, and not just give the right answer because they fear making a mistake.

If we are emphasizing true learning, we need to embrace effort and accept that mistakes are part of the package. We need to ask what lessons can be learned from a mistake. We should praise not only the grade a student earns, but also the process of thinking the student followed to achieve that grade. Mis-takes should not define a person, but instead should serve as a springboard, through self-assessment and reflection, to new ideas and plans of action. Our focus should not solely be on the "right" answer or the "correct" way of doing something but also on the risk or effort students exhibit on their journey of learning.

The following activities are included in this section:

- **Get Back Up Again**
- **Famous Failures**
- **Oops!**
- **The Blame Game**

Get Back Up Again

Social Skills: Through the course of this activity, students will demonstrate their ability to focus on a task and take alternative steps (alter their environment) to overcome difficulties.

Executive Functions: Students will demonstrate grit by trying very hard, even if they are experiencing failure. Students also will show self-control by focusing on the tasks.

MATERIALS NEEDED

- *GRIT & Bear It!* book
- Rewards for those who extend their time on the third trial of the wall activity
- "Get Back Up Again Twitter Board" (a long piece of butcher paper displayed somewhere in the room that allows you to post and erase different messages throughout the year; choose a width that can go through a laminator)
- Markers (non-permanent) for writing on the "Get Back Up Again Twitter Board"

- Computer
- Timer
- Graph paper (or access to online graphing software)
- Paper
- Pencils
- Visual of the social skill, "Focusing on a Task"
- Visual of the social skill, "Altering Your Environment"

Explain to the students that one of the characteristics of grit is the ability to rebound after a setback. Everyone encounters setbacks and small failures as they pursue goals. However, individuals who possess grit have resiliency. They can overcome obstacles and get back up after being knocked down.

DIRECTIONS

1. Review with students the steps of the skill, **"Focusing on a Task"**:

   a. **Think about the task.**

   b. **Stay with the activity.**

   c. **Ignore distractions from others.**

2. Ask students to stand with their back against a wall. Have them slide down the wall until they are in a sitting position (minus the chair!). Ask them to hold that position for as long as they can or for a set amount of time. Have students time and record on a piece of paper how long they can hold that position. The last student to stand up wins.

3. Have the students repeat the activity. This time, ask them to improve on their time. Have students record their new time when they finish.

4. Ask the students to perform the activity a third time, again encouraging them to beat their previous times. Have them record their times again, and reward the students who improve their time.

5. Have students graph the three times they wrote down during the activity, either on graph paper you provide or online. Do not tell them what type of graph to construct; let them pick one that they feel best represents the information. Have them share their graphs and defend their choices.

6. Ask students if they displayed grit. Help them understand that even if they did not achieve better times each time they did the activity, they still showed grit by trying it a second and third time.

7. Write the following quote by Dylan William on the board:

   "Greatness is often achieved after repeated failure."

   Have students write down what they think this quote means and how it relates to grit. Have students share their assessments with the class.

8. Ask students how Dylan William's quote applies to them in school, in their family, and in competitions.

9. Review the *GRIT & Bear It!* book with the class. Show page 17 and ask students how long they think it takes to put out wildfires. Ask them if firefighters are always successful the first time. What would happen if they didn't try again?

10. Show a video clip of someone overcoming an obstacle or portraying grit. A video clip of Derek Redmond running the 400-meter sprint in the 1992 Barcelona Olympics is a

good example of an individual displaying grit in order to finish a race. Ask students to reflect on how difficult it would have been to finish that race. Encourage them to share their thoughts and opinions.

11. Ask students to write down one way they will get back up again in one activity or one area of their life. Ask them to also share this information as a written "tweet" on the class "Get Back Up Again Twitter Board."

12. Introduce the "Get Back Up Again Twitter Board" (the butcher paper you have laminated and displayed) and explain that it works like a Twitter feed. As part of their grade, you could require students to tweet something once a week about grit or how they are developing more grit, using twitter language and symbols.

13. Have each student write down and hand in an identifying name so you can track their comments each week without other students knowing who wrote a comment. (Or use whatever method makes it easiest for you to monitor the comments.) The board serves as a constant visual reminder of how students are developing and displaying grit.

14. Explain to students that this activity will require them to use the skill of **"Altering One's Environment"**:

    a. **Identify situations in which you encounter difficulty.**

    b. **Look for parts of those situations that could be changed to bring about improvement.**

    c. **Make appropriate changes to improve self-esteem, behavior, or performance.**

To prevent sore muscles the next day, make sure students don't stay in the "chair" position too long while doing the wall activity.

Flipped Classroom: Post video links, either online or on the class website/blog, about individuals who "Get Back Up Again" when facing difficulties. Ask students to watch the videos and write down three ways they "Got Back Up Again." Have students share their lists in class.

Additional Resources: Examples of "tweets" or instructions for using Twitter for students who might not have used it before.

Famous Failures

Social Skills: Students will practice gathering information and persevering on the task of writing a survival guide.

Executive Functions: Students will understand that many famous people displayed grit when they continued to try very hard even after experiencing failure.

MATERIALS NEEDED

- Articles/Links about famous people who failed many times before finally succeeding
- Poster paper
- Colored pencils
- Access to the Internet

- Visual of the social skill, "Gathering Information"
- Visual of the social skill, "Persevering on a Task"
- "Success Survival Guide" sample

DIRECTIONS

1. Ask students to research the life of a famous person who failed before finally finding success. (See the list of possible examples on the next page.) Ask students to include information on how many times the person failed, how he or she failed, whether or not anyone discouraged him or her, obstacles the person faced, and other difficulties the person may have had to overcome.

2. Remind students of the steps of the skill, **"Gathering Information"**:

    a. **Know the topic and information needed.**

    b. **Use appropriate books or online search engines.**

    c. **Assemble materials, asking for help when needed.**

    d. **Write down the information needed.**

3. Ask the students to write down anything their famous person did to turn failure into success. Ask them to look for steps the person took to continue his or her pursuit of success.

4. After making sure the students know exactly what must be done, remind them of the steps of the skill, **"Persevering on Tasks and Projects"**:

    a. **Know exactly what must be done. Be sure to ask questions if you are unsure.**

    b. **Get started right away.**

    c. **Remain on task even if it takes longer than expected to complete.**

    d. **Appropriately deal with frustrations or disappointments.** *(Remind students that they develop grit when they can overcome frustrations and keep working.)*

5. If students have access to computers, have them create an electronic version of a "Success Survival Guide" that others could follow, based on the steps their famous people took. (See the example at the end of this activity.) These guides should include information about the famous person and pictures. Otherwise, have students create their survival guides using poster paper and colored pencils.

6. Have students print their guides and share them with the class. If possible, have the guides mounted so they can be displayed around the classroom or building. Students may find that writing out the steps for their guides will require perseverance, and they may have to revise their steps several times.

Create an example of a "Success Survival Guide" for students to view. This will make it clear what you are asking them to do.

Flipped Classroom: Ask students to view several on-line accounts of famous people who have failed. Provide several links for students to explore. Students can pick one person and provide the information requested in Step 1 about him or her before coming to class. Students should use class time to plan and develop their survival guides based on the failures and successes of that famous person.

FAMOUS PEOPLE WHO FAILED BUT PERSEVERED

Albert Einstein	Michael Jordan	Abraham Lincoln	Bill Gates
Walt Disney	Steve Jobs	Steven Spielberg	Marilyn Monroe
Oprah Winfrey	The Beatles	JK Rowling	Eminem

Additional Resources: Additional background information on famous people who failed before they found success.

WHAT IS A SUCCESS SURVIVAL GUIDE?

Discuss this question for a few moments and lead students to the following conclusion: Just like we might need a survival guide to stay alive in the desert or the wilderness, we also might need a "Success Survival Guide" to keep our goals and dreams alive when obstacles and setbacks threaten to defeat us.

Tell students:

After you have read about your "Famous Failure" and listed the obstacles he or she faced, start making a list of the steps that person took to overcome those obstacles and setbacks in order to reach his or her goal(s). How did he or she succeed? What would his or her "Success Survival Guide" have looked like?

Include at least three pictures for each step of your "Success Survival Guide."

Then show students an example of a "Success Survival Guide," like the one printed below for Harlan David Sanders. Have students complete a guide for their person.

Success Survival Guide

FAMOUS FAILURE: _Harlan David Sanders_

Obstacles the person faced:_____

father died at age 6; had to care for younger siblings at age 10; had to work many jobs to support his family; new business ruined by a highway development; had to start over at age 65

STEP 1: "GET GOING EVEN IF IT'S HARD!"

When Harlan David Sanders was 6, his dad died.

At age 10, Harlan had to cook and care for his younger siblings.

He also held several jobs.

Harlan did not feel sorry for himself.

STEP 2: "GOT BACK UP AGAIN"

Had a successful gas station, with chicken dinner "home meal replacements."

Opened Sanders Café with his secret recipe. Governor of Kentucky made him "Colonel of Cuisine."

In 1955, a new highway ruined his business.

Even though he was 65, he got back up and traveled the country selling franchises for his chicken.

STEP 3: "NEW ENERGY - KEEP GOING!"

Traveled the country to recruit small restaurants as franchises.

Cooked for them and sold recipe for 5 cents per chicken sold.

Ten years later, he had sold 600 franchises.

He sold his company for $2 million.

His face is on KFC.

Lesson Extension: How can you take the lessons from your "Famous Failure" and apply them to your own "Success Survival Guide"? Select an area that you have already succeeded in or one in which you need to keep working and begin writing your own "Success Survival Guide." Remember to include pictures for the steps you are taking or could take to help you succeed.

Oops!

Social Skills: Students will learn positive ways to deal with failure.

Executive Functions: Students will continue to try hard even after realizing they are failing at the activity.

MATERIALS NEEDED

- Drawing paper
- Markers or colored pencils
- Visual of the social skill, "Dealing with Failure"

- 10-15 items that were invented because of a mistake (see suggestions on the next page)
- A summarized history of each item and how it came into existence

DIRECTIONS

1. Bring in 10-15 items that exist today because of a mistake someone made and set them on a table for the students to view.

2. Ask the students to examine the items and then decide what all of them have in common. Give the students several minutes individually and then several minutes in small groups to figure out the answer. (They probably will not be able to figure it out.)

3. Tell the students that all of the items are similar because they were discovered through a mistake or by accident. Give a brief history of each item.

4. Have the students think of several ways each item has been beneficial in their daily lives, even though it was invented by mistake.

5. Ask students to write down the names of the items they think were the greatest "mistakes" and the one they consider to be the best "mistake." Have them support their choices.

6. Give each student a piece of drawing paper and a marker, and ask them to draw one of the "invention mistakes" in detail. The catch is they can't look at their paper while drawing or use their erasers if they make a mistake. If they make a mistake, they must continue drawing, which could turn the actual object into something new and different. When they are finished, have them look at their papers and ask them how it felt to know they were making some mistakes, or if they knew they were making mistakes. Work toward getting the answer

that it bothered them. Then tell them there are positive ways they can deal with failure, and go over the steps of the skill, **"Dealing with Failure"**:

  a. **Identify that you didn't succeed.**

  b. **Stay calm and control your emotions.**

  c. **Find a caring adult and talk about your disappointment or negative feelings.**

  d. **Be willing to try again.**

7. Have the students color their "new" object drawings in a fun and creative way, hopefully turning it into a completely new "invention mistake."

8. Post the drawings around the room under the heading, "Mistakes of Today Will Be Visions of Tomorrow!" Tell the students that these will be visual reminders of how it is okay to make mistakes, learn from them, and become better!

Encourage the students to use their creativity to develop their own "invention mistake." This reinforces their understanding of the concept that even if they don't do something perfectly, or even correctly, they can still produce something good, if not better, by persevering through their mistakes.

Flipped Classroom: Post 10-15 "invention mistakes" on your class website or blog. Ask the students to determine what the items have in common before class the following day. Have them write down their answer, with reasons to support it, and be ready to turn it in as they enter class the next day.

Additional Resources: Detailed information for each "invention mistake" example listed here.

1. Post-It-Notes
2. Silly Putty
3. Slinky
4. Potato Chips
5. Penicillin
6. Chocolate Chip Cookies
7. Pacemaker
8. Microwave Oven
9. Fireworks
10. Cornflakes
11. Inkjet Printer
12. X-rays
13. Ice Cream Cone
14. Popsicle
15. Velcro

The Blame Game

Social Skills: Students will practice self-correcting their behavior and take responsibility for their actions.

Executive Functions: Students will explore the idea that effort, not blaming others, will improve their future.

MATERIALS NEEDED

- *GRIT & Bear It!* book
- 2 signs that read, "I made a mistake."
- 2 jars, one labeled Jar 1 and the other Jar 2
- Slips of paper
- Links to video clips that demonstrate not blaming others or circumstances

- Pencils
- Paper
- Visual of the social skill, "Taking Responsibility"
- Visual of the social skill, "Self-Correction"

DIRECTIONS

1. Show the students the two jars. On the outside of each jar, attach a sign that says, "I made a mistake."

2. To begin the activity, hand out slips of paper to all the students. Ask the students to think about an actual mistake they've made and have them write as many negative things about that mistake as they can think of on the slips of paper (one negative thing per slip). For example, they might write: "I'm going to quit"; "Nothing ever goes my way"; "It was my sister's fault"; "I didn't feel good"; and others. (Make sure there are several negatives about blaming others.) Have the students place all of their slips of paper in Jar 1.

3. Next, ask students to think about all the positive ways they could view a mistake and write those down on slips of paper (one positive way per slip). These could include: "I think I can learn something here"; "I will try harder next time"; "I will make a new plan"; "I know I can do this"; "Mistakes are opportunities"; and others. Have the students place all those slips in Jar 2.

4. Tell the students the jars represent their minds. One jar is full of negative thoughts about mistakes, while the other is full of positive thoughts about mistakes.

5. Ask for two volunteers.

6. Have the first volunteer come up, pull a paper from Jar 1, and read it to the class.

7. Then have the second volunteer come up, pull a paper from Jar 2, and read it to the class.

8. Explain to the students that what we put in our minds is what we get out! If you tell yourself all these negative things about mistakes and blame others, then you're likely to get negative results. However, if you put positive thoughts about mistakes in your mind, then you're likely to get positive results. We have a choice! One will keep you stuck, and the other will help you overcome failures and persevere.

9. Discuss the following questions with students:

    a.   Have you ever blamed others for your mistake? Explain.

    b.   When are you most likely to blame someone else?

    c.   How can you stop doing that?

    d.   Are you taking responsibility for your own actions when you blame others?

10. Introduce students to the steps of the skill, **"Taking Responsibility"**:

    a.   **Accurately identify your own role in an event or situation.**

    b.   **Remain calm.**

    c.   **Analyze the situation to determine if it needs to be reported.**

    d.   **Avoid making excuses or blaming others.**

    e.   **Accept earned consequences calmly.**

11. Tell students that if they feel like blaming someone else for their failures, they should use the skill of **"Self-Correction"** instead:

    a.   **Be aware of your behavior during a difficult situation.**

    b.   **Notice how your behavior is affecting others and what their responses are.**

    c.   **Instruct yourself to correct the behavior that is making others uncomfortable.**

    d.   **Use a new behavior and note the effects.**

    e.   **Continue to make adjustments.**

    f.   **Reward yourself for correcting your behavior.**

Explain to students that when they self-correct their behavior instead of blaming others, they are taking responsibility for their own actions.

12. Review the *GRIT & Bear It!* book with the class. Draw the students' attention to page 27, with the dancer. Remind the class that taking responsibility and self-correcting help form character.

13. Ask students to practice self-correction with a partner. They can start by blaming their partner for something, then stop and use the steps of "Self-Correction" they have learned.

14. Show a video clip of a movie where a character is encouraged not to blame others for his or her failures or disappointments. The movie "Rudy" has a good example of this in a scene where the custodian confronts Rudy when he decides he is going to quit the football team because he won't get to play in the final game. Ask students to write down the advantages they will have if they persevere and show grit through a mistake or failure, instead of blaming others and quitting.

There are several current movies you can use to show the value of not blaming others and not giving up. If you are utilizing the Flipped Classroom suggestions, make sure to preview video links before showing them in class. Be sure to follow Fair Use laws when showing videos.

Flipped Classroom: Have students locate a video clip of someone who wants to blame others or circumstances for his or her failures, but instead overcomes this temptation and perseveres through the difficulty. Ask them to send a link to you by email for class the following day.

Additional Resources: Other video clips that focus on persevering and showing grit, rather than blaming others and quitting.

APPENDIX

Social Skills List

SECTION 1

Following Instructions

1. Look at the teacher while instructions are being given.

2. Say "Okay," or smile and nod your head.

3. Do what you've been asked to do right away.

Doing Good Quality Work

1. After receiving the instructions, assemble the necessary materials and tools.

2. Carefully begin working while focusing your attention on the task.

3. Continue working until the task is completed.

4. Examine your work, correct any deficiencies, and check back with the teacher.

Persevering on Tasks and Projects

1. Know exactly what must be done. Be sure to ask questions if you are unsure.

2. Get started right away.

3. Remain on task even if it takes longer than expected to complete.

4. Appropriately deal with frustrations or disappointments.

SECTION 2

Waiting Your Turn

1. Sit quietly, while waiting your turn, and remain still.

2. Avoid begging, whining, or making other noises while waiting.

3. Engage in the activity when asked to do so.

4. Thank the person who gives you a turn.

Staying On Task

1. Look at the task or assignment.

2. Think about the steps that are needed to complete the task.

3. Focus all your attention on your task.

4. Stop working on the task only if given permission by the adult who gave you the task, or if you reach your goal.

5. Ignore distractions and interruptions by others.

Choosing Appropriate Words to Say

1. Know the meaning of the words you are going to use.

2. Avoid using words that would offend someone or would be confusing. Also refrain from using slang, profanity, or words with a sexual meaning.

3. Then, make a decision on the words to use and write them down.

Assessing Your Own Abilities

1. Make a list of your strengths and weaknesses.

2. List situations in which you have been successful or have had problems.

3. Plan future activities in consideration of your abilities.

Analyzing Tasks to Be Completed

1. Clarify the goal.

2. List the steps needed to achieve that goal and what will be required to accomplish each step.

3. Put the steps in order.

4. Write down all suggestions (be sure to include your own ideas).

Setting Goals

1. **"Dream It."** Decide on your goal. Set high goals, and think about your values and desires.

2. **"Plan It."** Write down the sequence of steps needed to achieve the goal. List any resources you will need.

3. **"Work It."** Write out a "working" plan. Examine each step and allow time for steps that may take longer or require more work.

4. **"Endure It."** Write down what you will do if you get frustrated or experience a setback or an obstacle. Remain flexible so you can adapt your steps to changing circumstances.

5. **"Own It."** Write down the date you will "own" your goal, and what emotions you think you will have.

SECTION 3

Contributing to Discussions/Talking with Others

1. Look at the person who is talking.

2. Wait for a time when nobody else is talking (avoid interrupting).

3. Use a pleasant voice.

4. Choose words that are not offensive or confusing.

5. Make a short, appropriate comment that is related to the topic, or ask questions.

6. Allow others to speak.

Task Analysis

1. Clarify what the task or assignment is.

2. List every step.

3. Identify the steps in order.

4. Make a plan to begin.

Altering One's Environment

1. Identify situations in which you encounter difficulty.

2. Look for parts of those situations that could be changed to bring about improvement.

3. Make appropriate changes to improve self-esteem, behavior, or performance.

Listening to Others

1. Look at the person.

2. Sit or stand quietly and refrain from fidgeting or giggling.

3. Wait until the speaker has finished before you ask questions.

4. Show you understand by nodding your head or by telling the speaker you appreciate him or her being there.

SECTION 4

Delaying Gratification

1. Identify the want.

2. Tell yourself you can wait for what you want (e.g., candy).

3. Remain calm and relaxed.

4. Find ways or activities to focus your attention. Avoid thinking about getting the reward or payoff right away.

Rewarding Yourself

1. Decide if what you did was praiseworthy.

2. If so, tell yourself that and feel good about it.

3. Give yourself an extra privilege or reward.

4. Prompt yourself to increase your competency and ability.

Displaying Effort

1. Remain on task and work diligently.

2. Do your best.

3. Remember to inform the teacher before you move on to a new task.

SECTION 5

Focusing on a Task

1. Think about the task.

2. Stay with the activity.

3. Ignore distractions from others.

Altering One's Environment

1. Identify situations in which you encounter difficulty.

2. Look for parts of those situations that could be changed to bring about improvement.

3. Make appropriate changes to improve self-esteem, behavior, or performance.

Gathering Information

1. Know the topic and information needed.

2. Use appropriate books or online search engines.

3. Assemble materials, asking for help when needed.

4. Write down the information needed.

Persevering on Tasks and Projects

1. Know exactly what must be done. Be sure to ask questions if you are unsure.

2. Get started right away.

3. Remain on task even if it takes longer than expected to complete.

4. Appropriately deal with frustrations or disappointments.

Dealing with Failure

1. Identify that you didn't succeed.

2. Stay calm and control your emotions.

3. Find a caring adult and talk about your disappointment or negative feelings.

4. Be willing to try again.

Taking Responsibility

1. Accurately identify your own role in an event or situation.

2. Remain calm.

3. Analyze the situation to determine if it needs to be reported.

4. Avoid making excuses or blaming others.

5. Accept earned consequences calmly.

Self-Correction

1. Be aware of your behavior during a difficult situation.

2. Notice how your behavior is affecting others and what their responses are.

3. Instruct yourself to correct the behavior that is making others uncomfortable.

4. Use a new behavior and note the effects.

5. Continue to make adjustments.

6. Reward yourself for correcting your behavior.